Table of Contents

The essential guide to writing a business plan like a professional

Introduction

Whether you are starting a new business from scratch, developing your business for growth, buying a business, or buying a franchise, in all cases, a business plan is required. A business plan helps business owners to anticipate the potential market for their product or service. It also prepares them the costs involved for satisfying their customers, prepare them for potential pitfalls, and they can watch out for any warning signals of failure.

A business plan is there to demonstrate what the business intends to do. It shows its projected earnings and expenses and how the owner intends to repay any loans that were used to finance the business. Therefore, the business plan forces the business owner to answer the following questions: where is the business going and how will it get there? What problems is the business likely going to run into and how will you deal with it?

Thus a business plan becomes a roadmap which tells the owner how to get from one point to another within a certain period (usually between 12 months and 5 years). This is the reason why it's an important document for the owner as it helps them appreciate what it takes to succeed. It's also essential to investors to enable them to decide whether to assist through financing or not.

If you have a great business idea and want to raise enough capital, the best way is to have a comprehensive business plan. It's only through this way that potential investors can get an insight into the real value of your business. To achieve a profitable venture, you will need to understand how to grow your business, when are you going to launch your products or services, who else is going to be involved, and how you will manage the company's finances.

Once you have realized the importance of a business plan, and why you need to create one, then it's time to engage in the actual writing of the document. However, writing a business plan is one of the most challenging tasks for business owners. Hence, this guide will take you through the key steps in writing a good business plan to help you achieve your goals. It will allow you to refine strategies by examining your business from all perspectives, including finance, marketing, and operations. When you use the tips included in this guide, your business plan will boost your confidence in operating the business and achieving your goals.

Chapter 1: Things to consider before preparing a business plan

Document all aspects of your business

Whether you have been in business for a few months or a couple of years, an infusion of funds into your business is always welcome. Many business owners have tried to raise capital for their business and while some have succeeded, others have not done well. Potential investors and lenders are usually interested to see whether your business is a viable venture or not. Because of this expectation, they try to know every aspect of your business. To help them evaluate the risks and returns, you need to document everything from your strategic plans, operational plans, financial plans, and industry projections. Below are the specific details that you need to prepare for your business:

1. Strategic plans

When it comes to funding, the first things that come to mind for most business owners are the investors and lenders. People have to keep in mind that there is a human being at the end of any paper trail. Whether it's a bank or private investor, the person reading your business plan will have to determine if it's worth it to invest in your business. Therefore, you have to formulate a strategic plan that suits the market conditions. This means you need to use a clear company's mission statement and vision statement so that will attract and motivate both your employees and other people reading your plan. While the strategic plans articulate the direction the business is going, mission and vision statements communicate the goals of that strategic plan to either employees or the public.

Investors, lenders, partners, customers, and employees want to see the mission statement that states the purpose and measurable objectives of your business. In the same way, the vision statement is there to describe the purpose of your business. When you include the vision statement in your business plan, it will inspire them. For the consumers, they might be encouraged and inspired to work with your company. A business plan without a vision statement gives investors and lenders a sign that your business has no purpose and lacks an idea of how it would succeed. Below are great examples of a mission statement and vision statement:

Mission statement: We offer a variety of well-designed, functional office desks at the lowest possible prices and the uttermost convenience.

Vision statement: To create a better everyday life for people at workplaces.

2. Operational plans

An operational plan has detailed information to guide people when performing their day-to-day duties needed in the running of your business. It's not surprising that the management and staff usually refer to the operational plan in carrying out their routine tasks. It gives information on what tasks and strategies need to be done, who should perform such tasks and strategies, when the tasks and strategies should be completed, and the amount of financial resources required to complete the tasks and strategies. The employees performing the tasks and strategies refer to the operational plan to get a clear picture of their responsibilities and duties in line with the goals, mission, vision, and objectives as articulated in the strategic plan.

When you include operational plans in your business plan, investors and lenders will see that you have everything in place to achieve success. The operational plan should be flexible enough to enable you to adjust it as the business grows, and as you get to know better your customers and competitors. This will be the only way the plan can remain useful. The following table is a simple operation plan you can use for your business.

Strategies/ Objectives	Time frame	Person Responsible
Conduct visits to customers	Four visits per week to selected companies	Marketing Manager
Advertise major events through social media and print media	Adverts placed in business's social media platform and national newspapers in July, August, and September.	Events Coordinator
Initiate a campaign to acquire corporate clients	The campaign starts August and finishes in October	Sales Team Leader
Conduct social events targeting schools	Events to be done every four months	Promotions Team Leader
Hiring Outside Vendors for competitor research	To be done quarterly: January, April, July, and September	Marketing Research Manager
Review and approve time for staff reporting for work.	To be done every day when staff report for duties	Functional Managers
Notifying the Project Manager about possible project risks	Four meetings every month	Project Team Leaders
Hiring new employees	Once every year or when there is	HR Manager

	a vacancy	
Review project progress documents	To be done every month	Business Partners
Allocate financial resources and work packages	To be done every month	Finance Manager

3. Financial plans

Investors and lenders are keen to see the financial statements and financial projections of your business. In particular, they want to find out that you created milestones and formulated the right tools to measure the progress of your business. Besides trying to know your budget on various aspects of your business, investors want to see your management team and make sure that you have the right talent to help your business succeed.

It's for these reasons why the financial section of your business plan has to incorporate the income statement, the cash flow projection, and the balance sheet. You will also need to come up with a brief analysis of the three statements.

Determining the purpose of the business plan

A business plan that clearly defines your vision, mission, how you will succeed, and how you will make money assures you or the investors that your business has direction. A good business plan will help you to focus on the necessary steps to take for your ideas to succeed and achieve both your short-term and long-term goals. However, excellent business ideas can fail if you cannot formulate and implement a strategic plan to make them work.

If you are looking to raise capital from institutional investors, you should keep in mind that you need a great business plan. The document should be able to speak for itself, meaning it has to be clear, easy to read and understand. Therefore, before writing a business plan, consider your target audience. For example, for raising capital for your business, your readers are the investors and lenders. On the other hand, for joint ventures or partnerships, the potential business partners will be your readers.

It's important to note that a business plan is there to stand for you, your business, and the promise you are making. It's your plan and outside writers cannot change this basic principle. But, if you are working within this fundamental principle, outside writing assistance can help with your business plan. If you have the resources, you can hire someone to review your business plan and your planning process. The person should have the industry experience, be capable of identifying any missing details, and determine if it's easy to read and understand. Some of the financial details can be challenging, but you can do them yourself with the assistance of an expert who can even coach you. An outside expert should just be there to guide you towards the key issues by highlighting the important points that you need to include in the business plan.

Alternatively, you can find someone from within your team to help you write the business plan. The person should be available for the long term, has relevant experience, and knows the industry pretty well. Think through the managers and other senior staff who are in your team, who can be available to assist you with the business plan.

Chapter 2: Formatting the business plan

The spacing and font size

The formatting of your business plan should be simple for easy reading by your readers. You can use the general formatting that has single spacing with an extra space between paragraphs. For example, you can use serif fonts such as Baskerville or Garamond. If your targeted audience is going to read the business plan on their computers, then sans serif fonts like Ariel or Verdana are probably the best choice.

The idea for choosing different fonts for off-screen and on-screen is because there is evidence suggesting that readers have a higher understanding when they read texts with a serif on paper. But, this is different from on-screen as most readers have a higher apprehension when you use a sans serif font.

While you can choose any of the above four fonts, ensure that the font size is either 10 or 12-point to make it readable. It's not ideal to decrease the font size to reduce the length of the business plan as it will only make the texts difficult to read. Instead, cut down the content included in the plan. As for the margins, you can utilize one-inch margins to ensure the business plan is readable.

Cover pages

You can make your business appealing by including cover pages. This matters a lot because investors and lenders will start judging you by first looking at your presentation. Use the cover page to display your business name, business logo, and your value proposition. Here are other details you should consider including on the cover page:

- Company name - The first thing that you need to include on the cover of the business plan is the company's name. This should be a more prominent feature by ensuring that you use the largest font as much as possible. It helps the readers to immediately know the name of your business.
- Business color scheme and logo will enable your business plan not only to look the best but appear professional. Consider using a high-quality image of your business logo together with the right font type and color scheme. A cover with such features will instantly draw attention to the business plan
- The top page which is the first page should include the title of the business plan. The cover should show if it's a business plan, financial projections, or executive summary. Remember to write the date when the business plan was written so that the readers can know. You can include the actual month and year.
- Key contact information - The cover page should have the business address (both physical and postal addresses), names of directors (include their physical addresses), type of business (it can be transport business such as passenger and cargo haulage), type of business ownership (it can be sole proprietorship, partnership, or LLC), bankers, legal practitioners and auditors.
- At this stage your cover page will read **as illustrated in appendix, page 30, cover page.** Take note that the title of the business plan and the date should be less prominent than the name of your business.

When you present your business plan in the above stated standard business format with all the required business plan features, the potential investors and lenders are inclined to trust your business plan. Whether it's a banker or any other investor, they expect to see the necessary elements in your document, in the right order they expect to see it in. This also helps you to keep track of your presentation and save you from missing the best opportunity of getting the funds or support you are looking for.

Chapter 3: Business Description

The second page of your business plan is comprised of the company description. It usually comes after the executive summary which is the first page. The business description is a general description of your business and should give an outline of important elements of your venture, such as the location of the company, the size of the company, what the company does, and explain exactly what you want. The description also goes further by stating the vision, mission, and objectives of the business so that investors, lenders, and potential partners can have a clear picture of your company. The common elements to incorporate in the company description are the following:

- **The name of the business.** It should have the official business name as registered in the state where it's operating. You need to make sure that the name of your business is clear in the description.
- **The type of business.** This can be a law firm providing accident attorneys in a specific geographical location such as Culver City, California.
- **Type of ownership and management team.** The company's structure can be sole proprietorship, partnership, limited liability corporation, corporation, or LLC. You should mention what inspired you to form such a business structure and provide the names of key staff behind the business.
- **Location.** Investors are interested to know the location of the business. Therefore, mention the headquarters of the company.
- **Company history background/history.** State when the was launched and registered. For example, you

can explain that your business was formed in July 2019 and registered on September 2019. It's also important to mention your inspiration to start the business.

- **Mission statement.** A mission statement that is clear in explaining the purpose of your business will attract more attention. A mission statement should be unique to help you stand out from the competition.
- **Products or services and your target market.** Here you have to give a brief description of the products or services you offer. Consider mentioning the market you want to sell your products or services. This is the stage where you can outline your short-term and long-term goals for your products or services. If you plan to sell $50,000 of products by the end of the first year, include such details in your goals.
- **Objectives.** This is an overview of what you want to achieve in the short and long-term based on the information outlined in the business plan.
- **Vision statement.** A business with a vision statement demonstrates that the business owner has direction. Therefore, the statement should show your expectations for the business in the future.

After gathering all the key details that you want to include in the company description, it's now necessary to focus on writing appealing information. This means you should begin by writing a paragraph that will elevate the presentation. The paragraph should only contain crucial information about your business, meaning use a few sentences to explain the key details about your business.

If you are writing your company's description, you have to note that some of the information included in this section will also appear in the other sections of the document. For these parts, you have to write only high-level information and leave the specific details to be incorporated in their right sections.

A simple business description example

If you find it overwhelming writing a business description for your business plan, take a look at this example.

George Desks manufactures and supplies office desks to businesses in Culver City, Los Angeles. The business is a partnership, operating under George Smith and his wife, Jane Smith. George Desks is located in Culver City, California and started operating in January 2017.

The focus of George Desks has been to help businesses in need of office desks. Employees deserve comfortable workplaces considering their busy lives. The premises in Culver City is a testimony of the passion that the business has, it supplies various types of office desks to cater for local companies. George Desks will conveniently provide office desks to business owners who don't have enough time to shop around. Other office desks suppliers in the market cannot match this service.

The business hopes to achieve gross sales of $50,000 by the end of the first year and $150,000 by the end of five years. This goal will be achieved by selling office desks to customers who want them using a credit facility.

Chapter 4: Market analysis and demand estimation

The market analysis and demand estimation are the key components of your business plan. Investors and lenders will mostly judge your expertise in your industry and the attractiveness of the business from a financial perspective. The market analysis should have clear objectives to convince the potential investors and lenders that you have a viable business. You should demonstrate that you are familiar with the market and the market is good enough to create a successful business. Therefore, the market analysis should include demographics and market segmentation, target market, and competition.

Demographics and market segmentation

From the onset, try to estimate the size of the market. But, your approach in assessing its size will depend on the type of business you are operating. If you are operating a small passenger van rental business that is targeting local customers, then you will assess the local market around where your business is located. On the other hand, if you are operating a large passenger van rental business, then assess the market for your business plan at a national level.

The most critical factors to bear in mind when looking at the size of the market are the number of potential customers and the value the market brings to your company. Potential customers usually depend on the type of business. For example, if you have a local or small passenger van rental services, then your market will be all the people within your range of business.

However, estimating the market value can be tricky because of the challenges that come to get the information. It's important to find out if the data you are looking for is available publicly either through publications by a state body or a consultancy agency. If not, then the only way is to purchase market research reports or attempt to do an estimate yourself. The factors to consider when doing demand estimation are the following:

- When estimating your market share, you need to determine the size of the entire industry and market segment.
- You have to estimate competitors' market share.
- Determine how you would stand up against the competition.
- Estimate your sales volume.

Demand estimation

Two popular methods used in demand estimation are called the top-down approach and the bottom-up approach. In a top-down approach, you try to determine your market share by reducing it pro-rata the already known industry sales volume. For example, for a George Desks business in Culver City, California, you can start by finding the value of the office desks market in the United States, in this case, let's assume it's $500m. Then you can do a pro-rata on this figure using the number of companies operating in Culver City x their number of staff / total number of staff employed in the USA. You must note that the number of staff is just a rough figure because not all companies will require office desks for their employees.

When it comes to the bottom-up approach, the calculation is quite different because you start creating the market value in the United States using unitary values. In the example above, you take the number of potential customers and multiply it by an average value of the transaction. Therefore, to determine the office desks market value, you need to find out the size of the businesses within your area of operation. Then you will have to find the volume of annual transactions by keeping in mind the repurchasing rate. Lastly, take the average price times the annual volume of transactions to come up with the estimated market share. Here is how you can calculate it:

- Size of desks market = number of businesses in your area of operation x number of staff (you can adjust this figure because not all the staff require desks).
- Repurchase rate = 1/lifespan of an office desk
- The volume of transactions = size of front desks market x repurchase rate
- The market value = volume of transactions x the value of a single transaction

The best thing about the bottom-up approach is the fact that it's easy to get all the useful data. The number and size of companies operating in your geographical area can be obtained from the national statistics records while the accountant working in your company should be able to provide the lifespan of an office desk. There is also nothing wrong in getting some information from your competitors as long as you don't reveal that you want to compete with them.

Demand estimation requires you to try both the top-down approach and the bottom-up approach so that you can compare the results. If you find out that there is a huge difference in the figures, probably there is something wrong with your calculation.

Demand drivers

Potential investors and lenders are also interested to know what drives the customers to look for your products or services. This is the part where you need to show your expertise and knowledge of the market. There should be complete and crystal clear details of demand drivers. One way to explain what a driver means is by looking at baby disposable diapers. People look for consistency in accessing this product. The baby diapers you can buy from a supermarket are the same as the ones found in your local shops. However, customers who are not residents and are not familiar with the shops are not aware of this. Therefore, they opt to buy from the supermarket because they know that they will find the baby disposable diapers they are looking for just like any other supermarket in that company.

Target market

The target market is the specific segment of customers you intend to sell your products or services. For example, if you are selling roof repair services, you can either focus on residential homes or commercial property. This is a relevant section, especially if there are clear segments with different needs. For roof repair services, residential homes usually go for value for money whereas commercial properties are driven by the quality of the services.

Competition

There are various companies in the marketplace offering the same type of product or service. You have to explain who your business is competing against, your position in the market, competitors' strengths and weaknesses. It makes sense to analyze how your competitors approach the market so that you can identify the weaknesses that your business can capitalize on to its advantage. The best way to analyze your competitors is to look at the major market drivers. If you can place the results in a table, it will make it easier for you to compare all the competitors. While comparing the other companies, make sure that your business has a core competency. If you perform that core competency better than your competitors, then it becomes distinctive competency.

Chapter 5: Company's structure and management

The traditional saying that investors and lenders would rather invest in a talented team than ideas no matter how average the idea is still true today. It's a well-known practice that the right talent can build a business to become successful. It means that operating a successful business boils down to getting the work down. Therefore, investors would try to find out if you can achieve your plans by assessing the team you have hired. This is the only way you can get enough customers coming to purchase your products or services.

Important details to consider including

The company's structure and management team chapter of your business plan is the only section where you can show the potential investors and lenders that you have the right talent to accomplish your idea. This section should demonstrate that you have taken time to consider properly the key roles and responsibilities your company requires to develop and be successful. You have to include an organizational chart of your business and how the operations take place.

An organizational chart for your business allows you to see your company and how it will develop over time. Therefore, you can plan on the roles that you will need in the future and how to structure your team to make sure it's productive. You can include this organizational chart in the appendix of your business plan.

Write the list of positions and describe what each key team member such as directors, technical specialists, accountants, and salespeople perform their roles. It's important to highlight the relevant skills, experiences, and educational background of your team members. Likewise, make a case by supporting the team as the right one to turn the vision into reality.

Common mistakes

Most new business owners tend to make the mistake of assigning everyone on their team a senior management position to ensure the business plan is complete. The problem with this method is that they find it challenging as the company grows because some positions require people with specific experience and knowledge of the industry. Another drawback is that you restrict the future growth of roles when you start with everyone at the top of the hierarchy.

Investors and lenders don't need to see that your management team is complete to make their decision on funding your business. The management team that has gaps typically will help them to understand that you are still looking for the appropriate key personnel to fill the positions for your company to succeed. If this is the case, identify the gaps and show that you are searching for the right talent to fill certain positions.

Employment creation usually resonates well with most investors and lenders. Take this opportunity to describe the steps you are taking to expand your employees. Mention the number of staff you have employed as a result of your business and discuss new roles you want to fill in and why. Your business plan is all about the present and the future of your business.

Chapter 6: Describe your product or service

The product or service chapter of your business plan allows you to tell the readers what your business is going to provide to its customers. Your products or services have to show their quality, value, and benefits to the customers. You should ask yourself the following questions: what are you selling? What's so special about your product or service? How will your customers benefit from them? How is your product or service different from the ones offered by your competitors?

This is one of the chapters of your business plan that should excite potential investors, lenders, or partners, who are hoping to fund your company or work with you. Because of this, here is what you need to do to write an appealing section:

- **Explain why customers need your product or service.** If your product or service is a new concept or there is no one in the market offering it, you have to provide details about why people would want to purchase your product or service.
- **Highlight the key features of your product or service.** Your product or service is going to be in high demand only if it has unique features different from similar products or services in the market. Consider explaining its pricing or the unique services you provide.
- **Explain its benefits.** The features you highlight will demonstrate their benefits to consumers. If the feature of your service is faster service, it means the benefit

will be the opportunity for customers to get it at any time. Customers usually look for products or services that fulfil their needs. Hence, highlight how your product or service satisfies that need.

- **Showcase your knowledge, expertise, and experience**. You want to show your readers that you have a great understanding of your product or service. Demonstrate to them that you are also the best to offer it because of your education, expertise, and experience in the industry. This is the best time to share your awards and testimonials.
- **Don't use complex language for your product or service**. Talk use difficult terms. While you might know your product or service pretty well, your potential investors and lenders might not have the same knowledge. It's essential to use simple terms so that your readers can understand what you're offering.
- **Write as if you are presenting your product or service to your customer**. A business plan is there for you to sell it to investors and lenders. Make sure that the product or service chapter is customer-oriented. If what your business is selling can appeal to your readers, there is a good chance that customers will also like it.

An example of a good chapter with a description of the product would be of George Desks. It should provide a detailed description of the office desks that showcases the various types of all the desks. Before you write a detailed description, you should include a summary showing why your particular office desks are different from those of competitors. Here is a great example, *"George Desks provides five different types of office desks: an executive desk, typist desk, clerical desk, secretarial desk, and machine desk. Our wide range of desks is the main competitive advantage because we have a diversity of product offerings that our competitors are not offering the target market".*

Chapter 7: Marketing and sales strategy

Marketing and sales strategy is another important chapter of your business plan, which provides details of how you intend to sell to your target market. A great product or service means nothing if you can't get customers. This is the reason why you need an excellent marketing plan to find your customers, making this chapter very important for investors and lenders when deciding to give you funding for your business.

For any business, the biggest challenge comes when you try to build a good reputation as a credible provider of a product or service. This is why you need to take time to position your product or service. Simple research will help you to determine if there are a lot of people ready to become your customers, and how much they are willing to pay for them.

You have to know your market and competition to come up with the marketing and sales chapter. Make sure you have the right message for your product or service, pricing, and other marketing strategies you can use to increase sales. A marketing plan it's comprised of 5 Ps of the marketing mix, which are the product, price, promotion, place, and people. You can use this marketing mix to satisfy your customers with your products or services. It's also important for you to know how you would measure the success of your marketing campaign to make sure that there is added value to your business. Below are the marketing 5 Ps:

Product

You will need to write a good description of your products or services offered to your customers. This includes the features of the products or services, their functions, the benefits, and their differences to products or services offered by your competitors.

Price

Indicate your pricing strategies to enable you to achieve your expected profit margin. Write how you price your product or service while remaining competitive in the marketplace. For example, you can calculate the price by considering the fixed expenses, variable expenses, time invested, and your expertise to make sure you have the right price for your product or service. Let the reader know that your price is either lower or higher than your competition, and explain the reasons for such differences. Pricing strategy should correspond with your business position in the marketplace. For example, if you tell your customers that you provide high-quality office desks, the pricing should reflect that.

The place also called distribution

Another important information investors and lenders would want to know are where you sell your products or services, and how the customers will get them. This is the place where customers will see, sell, or distribute the products or services. In essence, when making distribution decisions, you should consider how the products will get to the target customers. The customers need to have easy access to your products or services by ensuring that they are available at the right time, at the right place, and in the right amount. For example, if you sell your products online and local stores, explain how much you expect to sell in each distribution point. You can point out that 70% are online sales and 30% are through local stores. Include the terms and costs of delivering the products, explain how you cover such expenses, shipping or labelling requirements, transaction process, and product return policies.

Promotion

To improve the sales of your products and services, you have to do promotions because they make your business get known to customers. Indicate the methods you are using to communicate with your customers on the product or services features and their benefits. If you are advertising, state the media you are utilizing, the percentage you have allocated for each advertising media, the costs involved to do the advertising, the return on investment gained through advertising. Importantly, let the readers know if you are using incentives such as coupons or public relations activities to attract customers. Promotions can cost a lot of money, making it a good idea to have break-even analysis before conducting them. You need to understand the value the customer will bring to your business to determine whether it's worth it to take them on board.

People

Employees and customers are what makes your business to grow. You can achieve the goals of your sales strategy if you have the salespeople who have the skills to sell your products or services. You also need satisfied customers to continue buying your products or services. Therefore, it's important to demonstrate in your business plan that you have incentives or training programs for the sales staff to empower them to deliver high-quality customer service. At this point, indicate how you measure customer satisfaction and explain in your business plan how you want your sales team to be perceived by your customers.

Evaluating marketing campaign

While making key marketing decisions, you should also consider to find out the strategies that are working and those that are not. It doesn't make sense to continue with the marketing tactics that are just not giving a return on your investment. The first step is to plan the marketing campaign and find ways of tracking it. The success of your business depends on this, therefore, each marketing campaign should be a well thought out and effective initiative. As with anything else that you present in the business plan, write in detail the channels you track, the marketing metrics you measure, and the methods you use to track the effectiveness of the marketing campaigns. You can keep track of your marketing by using various tools such as Google Analytics to measure your marketing search engine performance. Take a look at the following marketing effectiveness metrics:

Return on Investment (ROI) will show your readers how you measure sales revenue as a result of the marketing campaign. For example, if George Desks Company spends $10,000 on a marketing campaign that generates $30,000 in sales, the company's ROI is $$20,000 or 200%. This is one of the best key performance indicators your business can use to measure the effectiveness of marketing campaigns.

Chapter 8: Funding request

When it comes to the funding chapter of your business plan, it's for your good to go straight to the point. Investors and lenders already know the purpose of your business plan, and you can make their job easier by making it simple for them to figure out what you are asking for. If you make it difficult for your readers to understand your funding request, there is a high chance that your request will be denied. This is why you need to include the following in the funding request section:

- Ask for the full amount you require for your business. Indicate if you want this amount of money in one lump sum, or you need the investor or lender to make further funding over time. Take into consideration the size of the amount of money you are asking for.
- State whether you want this funding to be regarded as a loan or investment. Do your research because both a loan and an investment have their benefits and disadvantages. Your decision will depend on what works best for your business. For instance, most investors will be looking for a shareholding in your business while lenders such as banks want a monetary return on the loan they provide.
- The banks have their terms you need to satisfy for your business to secure a loan. These terms will usually be agreed upon between you and the banks even before submitting your business plan. When this happens, make sure to include all the details they have asked you to write, but at all times, make sure that the terms and condition are favorable to your business.

The funding request should have the support of the financial statement that highlights cash flow statement, income statement, and balance sheet. If you don't have the proper educational background and experience, consider hiring an accountant, lawyer, or other experts to complete this part accurately. The financial statements are included in the appendix of your business plan.

Cash flow statement

The cash flow statement will show how your business tracks the money that is in the bank. A cash flow statement will point out the money you have on hand, adds the money you get through cash sales and paid invoices, and subtracts the cash expenses such as the money you pay for taxes, bills, and paying off loans. This will provide you with the total cash flow and your ending cash.

The good thing about the cash flow is that it gives potential investors and lenders a clear picture about the time you might have low or high reserves of cash. It also helps you to figure out the amount of money you might need to request from investors to grow your business. The cash flow statement should include all the transaction done each month with the annual total. You should include cash flow for at least 5 years or until the business establishes stable growth rated. A simple cash flow statement from operating activities using a direct method will look like this:

Cash from operating activities	
Cash received from customers	$ 10,000
Expenses using cash (subtractions):	
Cash paid for inventory	$ 1,000
Cash used for the insurance	$800
Cash used for selling expenses	$ 200
Taxes paid	$ 1,000
The net cash from Operating Activities	$ 7,,000

Income statement

The income statement is where you indicate if your business is making a profit or a loss. You can get the data from the sales forecast, personnel plan, and other expenses related to the operation of your business. It has all the expenses subtracted from all your income to indicate whether your business is making profits or losses each month. The profit and loss statement includes the following details:

- Income arising from sales of your products or services.
- Cost of goods sold (COGS) for the products or cost of sales when you are dealing with services. You can get this figure from the sales forecast.

- Calculate the gross margin by subtracting the COGS from the sales figure. Alternatively, you can use this formula to get the gross margin % = Gross margin/sales x 100%.
- Operating expenses is another detail you can include. This figure is calculated by taking down all the expenses, excluding COGS, taxes, depreciation, and amortization. Instead, include salaries for your staff, marketing expenses, and all other expenses.
- Total operating expenses are the total amount of all your operating expenses.
- Calculate the operating income also called earnings before interest, taxes, depreciation, and amortization (EBITDA). You can subtract all the operating expenses and COGS from the total sales.
- If you have interest, depreciation, taxes, and amortization, list them just below the operating income.
- Add your operating expenses to the interest, depreciation, taxes, and amortization to find your total expenses.
- To know that your business is making a profit or a loss, you have to show the net profit each month and for the year.

You should also do an income statement using accounting software. However, there is no single format because it varies depending on the type of business you are doing. In general, all income statements begin by showing the sales, followed by expenses, and the profits or losses come last. Here is what you should include in an income statement:
- **Revenue**. This is the money your business receives after selling your products or services.

- Cost of goods sold. This figure is for the direct cost of manufacturing the products offered by your business.
- Gross Profit. This is the difference you get from the revenue received for selling your product less the expenses on goods sold.
- Operating expenses. This is an amount your business spends to run it. It includes marketing expenses research and development, and administration expenses.
- Operating income. You can get this figure by subtracting the cost of goods and operating expenses from revenues.
- Other income or expenses. You can get net income if you adjust income tax expenses, interest income and expenses, and other miscellaneous items.
- Profits/losses. You can arrive at this figure by subtracting all expenses from revenues.

Balance sheet

The last financial statement that your business plan has to create is the balance sheet. It contains a brief analysis of the financial situation of your business. Consider incorporating the assets for the business, liabilities, and the business owner's equity. You can get the net worth of the business by subtracting the liabilities from the assets.

Security

Most of the businesses get funding from the banks, which usually provide loans by charging interest. You can take a loan from your bank and pay it back perhaps in instalments. The amount you are supposed to pay back consists of principal and interest, or sometimes, only the interest followed by payment of the principal. While repaying the loan, you don't have to offer your company as security or collateral.

Some banks will ask to have minimal input on how to run your business to make sure that your business succeeds. This is because the banks are concerned about getting their money back plus a return on their loan. It's for this reason why most banks look for specific details including an explanation on why you need the funds for. Bankers are not interested in seeing the growth projections of your business. Rather, they want to find out the alternative way you can pay back the loan in case something goes wrong. This is where they might ask you for collateral.

Collateral would be something you or your business owns that the bank can seize to get back their money you have borrowed. This includes the equity you have in your home, equipment, machinery or inventory. Banks ask for collateral because they know that you are bound to work hard for your business to make it successful.

There is nothing to be intimated by bank financing. Most of the financial institutions prefer to finance businesses that are already operating, have adequate cash flow, and collateral. Once you have these things in place, your banker will rest assured that you can service and repay the total amount of the loan.

Exit strategy

There is a need to include the exit strategy for your business. This is a plan that you put in place in case the company achieves its growth strategy. Selling the business or paying off investors are options that need considering. Investors would want to find out if you are prepared to relinquish ownership and decide to sell your business to your competitor or sell it to the public. After all, they want to ensure that they get a return on their investment, and the only way out could be for you to accept selling it to another company. Although you don't have to put detailed information, you should still point out some businesses that might want to buy you out if you are successful.

Chapter 9: Loan repayment schedule

When your business intends to take a business loan from a bank, the money will usually be paid back annually or twice a year. These payments are called loan amortization. You can use a financial calculator or your bank to calculate a loan amortization schedule to help you analyze the amount of money you are supposed to repay the bank. An amortization schedule is comprised of a table with details of loan repayments. It has the amount of principal and the interest, that you pay annually until the loan is paid off at the end of its duration.

While these periodic payments are the same, when you start repaying the loan, the amount that you pay is usually the interest. Over time, the percentage of the payment you make on the interest reduces and the principal amount increases. The loan amortization schedule also shows that most of the periodic payment becomes principal over the years. When you pay off the loan in equal installments over its life, the debt is called to be amortized.

How to calculate the amortization schedule

There are many tools you can use to calculate an amortization schedule, but you need to be familiar with them to complete them accurately. An amortization schedule will have the following columns:

- Column 1. This will show the year for the outstanding loan.
- Column 2. This column will indicate the balance of the loan. This is where the balance reduces every year

depending on the equal amount of the principal that you pay on the loan.

- Column 3. This is the total payment that is calculated by adding interest paid to the principal paid.
- Column 4. Here it shows interest payments calculated as beginning balance x interest rate.
- Column 5. These are principal payments depicted as equal annual installments as requested by the lender.

Here is an example of an amortization schedule for a business loan of $50,000 at a 10% interest rate with a five-year term or life.

Year	Starting Balance	Total Paid	Interest Paid	Principal Amount Paid	Pending Balance
1	$50,000	$15,000	$5,000	$10,000	$40,000
2	$40,000	$14,000	$4,000	$10,000	$30,000
3	$30,000	$13,000	$3,000	$10,000	$20,000
4	$20,000	$12,000	$2,000	$10,000	$10,000
5	$10,000	$11,000	$1,000	$10,000	$0

The amortization schedule is there to let you know how much interest you are supposed to pay the lender over the term of the loan. If your business has a good cash flow, you can choose to pay off the loan early. You can do this by making a full prepayment or partial prepayments, ensuring that you save money which could have gone to payment of interest. It's important to read the conditions of your loan to find out if this provision is available, and if there are penalties or fees when you take the prepayment option.

Chapter 10: The executive summary

The executive summary is another decisive part of the business plan. It's a page or two that contains an overview of the main points included in your business plan, highlighting the major features. This is normally the first part of your business plan that potential investors and lenders will read first. Many people only ready the summary, whatever the case, while others will read the summary first to decide whether to continue reading or not. The readers will either want to keep reading or throw away your business plan. Therefore, getting the executive summary interesting and concise is crucial for your business if you are looking for funding.

The executive summary only has one purpose, and this is to explain the key features of your business plan in a way that will catch the attention of the reader. Yet you must include enough information to help investors and lenders see the potential behind your idea before reading the entire business plan. Because an executive summary is an overview of your business plan, make sure to leave readers with the confidence that the business is well-run, has direction, and there is a chance for success. The executive summary should include the following details:

- Explain who you are by writing the business's name, its location, and contact details.
- Include what the business offers and the problem your business intends to solve. Here you can write the product or service description and why it will benefit your customers. Products or services have to solve a need in the market or they are there when you find an opportunity.

- A brief description of your product or service will help the reader to understand what you are offering your target market.
- State the business plan purpose. You must say whether you are looking to secure a bank loan or you want investment.
- Mention that you are a business already operating by highlighting recent annual sales and number of employees in the list form.
- Indicate some of the essential details that would have a huge impact on the reader such as the founder holds an MBA degree from the local University. You can also mention that your business was awarded a prestigious recognition for creating employment.

It's important to note that not all business plans require an executive summary. An executive summary is critical if your business plan's purpose is to get funding from investors and lenders. However, if your business plan is only for internal use, then there is no need to write an executive summary because it's a huge task to do it.

How to write the perfect executive summary

The executive summary of your business plan should always be considered as a presentation with some restrictions. A great summary will grab the attention of the reader by summarizing the business plan. Readers have high expectations when reading your plan, and they want to see at least the business you are operating, your product or service, market, and financial details. You have to highlight all the information that you think will interest the reader so that your business plan can achieve its purpose. The following are some things you need to do when writing an executive summary:

- Write the executive summary last despite placing it at the beginning of your complete business plan. Ideally, the summary is supposed to be short covering a page or two pages. It should highlight the major points you have raised in your business plan.
- It should be short without skipping the essential points. If your executive summary is interesting enough, the readers will read the rest of the business plan where they can find all the information they are looking for.
- While outstanding executive summaries are short, they are also simply presented in bullets with subheadings.
- The subheadings should be discussed in the order of importance to demonstrate your emphasis. Begin writing the item that you want to grab the most attention, and follow with others in the order of importance.
- When you complete writing the executive summary, consider writing a summary memo. This is a short document you can attach to an email when sending to potential investors and lenders.

Make your business plan adaptable to your audience

There are various readers to your business plan such as venture capitalists, bankers, or employees. This is a diverse group, and each type of reader has a specific interest in your plan. If you have an opportunity to know the interest of your reader in advance, you can prepare your business plan to target that particular audience. For example, investors are looking for the basic business concept and the team you have, while the banks are more interested in your cash flow statement and balance sheets. The management team in your business want to see the business's objectives for direction. Because of this, ensure that your business plan is flexible enough for alterations depending on the target audience. However, these modifications should be minor ones. For instance, financial projections can remain the same from one business plan to another.

Executive summary targeting investors

An executive summary is probably the first part of your business plan that will convince prospective investors to fund your business. Time is of the essence, and most of your readers will have positive feelings about your business only if the executive summary is well-written. This means you should write it creatively, include only very important details, and get to the point.

You have a better chance of getting your business plan read if your executive summary is well-written. Investors receive a large number of business plans, and they usually only have time to read executive summaries before reviewing business plans later in the process. This means interesting summaries will go to the next stage where due diligence is conducted.

The summary should state clearly the amount of money you are trying to get and its use. This is just a summary because all the details will come elsewhere in your business plan. However, the first thing investors are interested to know is whether the amount you are seeking is within their capabilities. How you want to use the funds for will also make a huge difference. For example, it's less risky to ask for funding that will be used to purchase inventory for the orders you have already received. But, it's riskier to request for funds to develop a new product that is not in the market.

Valuation of your company is another important element. It says how much your business is worth in the market, this is a figure that will determine how much equity you offer for the potential investor. Valuation depends on investors because some of them only ask for summaries indicating the actual amount of money involved while others demand to do their valuation.

Your executive summary has to contain convincing facts which can be presented persuasively. You want prospective investors to keep reading and convince them to invest in your business. The content of your summary is what matters more than the tone. Facts should prove the availability of the target market or business experience.

Executive summary targeting banks

Investors might take risks on your business plan, but not banks. Banks are in the business of lending money, and to keep the reader interested, the executive summary has to cover major points of your business plan. They are going to look at the risk and return, such as stability of your business, financial history, assets displayed on the balance sheet, to determine the level of risk on the loan. When evaluating risk, banks will try and find out if you can service the loan. You have to prove that you have assets and sustainable cash flow to service the loan. It's against banking regulations for the banks to offer your business a loan without showing enough assets required to cover the value of that loan.

Most loan applications require you to provide a complete business plan because they want to understand your business.

The executive summary targeting lenders such as banks have to reassure that you are a suitable candidate for a loan. Hence what works well for the executive summary for investors doesn't work the same way for lenders. These are what bankers look for in your executive summary:

- Point out your net worth. Banks are interested to see your net worth as the business owner while investors are not. Investors are happy to see that you have a management team with business experience.
- Banks can assess the risk by looking at your past financial background and the bankable assets you possess. On the other hand, investors want to see the potential of growth for your business.
- Stability and how long you will stay in the market is what banks want to from their business borrowers.

If the bank shows interest in your business plan, they are going to invite you to explain the details you have included. This is great on your part because face-to-face presentations carry more weight. You must be ready to defend your business plan and include references to make your presentation even more credible. When you are looking for a loan, you should also take time to go through your entire business strategy and write this crucial thought process. Banks are also smart enough to detect a business plan that was written without a good plan.

Chapter 11: Finalizing your business plan

It's not a must to include an appendix at the end of your business plan. But, it's difficult to imagine a business plan without it because this section contains all the supporting documents that will make your case stronger. It clarifies and helps your readers to imagine what you have highlighted in the plan. These documents are important, but you have to include them in the very last chapter of your business plan. This is because combining them with the actual business plan might distract your readers from the key points you are trying to emphasize in the document. In essence, they tend to interrupt the natural flow of your presentation. Investors and lenders would want to see the information that supports your claims made in other chapters of your business plan before they make a decision.

An appendix should have documents to stress your best achievements and those of your management team. You can also decide to include resumes for your team. For example, in the body of your business plan, you can write, **"See Appendix, page 50, for resumes of the management team."** It's only in this way that you cannot disrupt the narrative of your business plan. Besides this, the reader can choose to keep reading your business plan without being interrupted and go to the appendix later on. They can also choose to stop reading and get to the page in the appendix to read the part you have referred them.

Option to skip an appendix

When writing your business plan, your intention should always be to write a concise and detailed plan that fulfils and addresses the readers' concerns or questions. The reader should not have to use the appendix because there are gaps, making it difficult to understand your business plan. The information included in the appendix is just supplementary and not formal.

The interests of readers vary because some readers might also be captivated by your narrative and want to make a good decision by checking what you have included in the appendix. For example, lenders might not find the credit history of your business in the main body not convincing. In this case, the appendix will be the first chapter they will read first.

You should do your best to present your appendix in a thoughtfully and creatively This will encourage the readers to read it and find the essential information they are looking for. The documents you include in the appendix should only be copies and not originals. Some of the documents you can include in the appendix are charts and graphs, competitor information, credit reports, incorporation papers, legal documents, letters of recommendation, pending contracts, pictures of your products, resumes of your management team, and tax returns. Remember to also attach some other important documents such as:

- Financial statements to show investors and lenders that the business is generating revenue.
- There should be a section in the appendix to indicate the risk factors for the business and the mitigation plans that are in place. This also shows the reader that you have prepared well with your contingency plans.

Conclusion

A business plan should include all the vital information, this makes proper organization skills crucial. With that in mind, you should realize that there is no definite rule available for writing a business plan. However, there are some basic sections you can follow to the letter depending on the audience such as a bank. The sections shared in the above guidelines are the most common ones and are well-received by a variety of audiences.

The perception you have when writing a business plan for your business is to demonstrate that your idea and venture is worth pursuing. It gives you the necessary details to help you achieve your goals. If there is anything to change considering the changing business environment, you can do it at an opportune time. A business plan also plays an integral part in presenting your company to prospective investors and lenders. This is the reason why you need to take a good look at the future of your business and how you are going to grow it.

Business plans can be written by individual owners if you're the sole owner or together with other partners in case of the business with several owners. It's important to note that this document is not only for internal use because you can use it to attract investors, lenders, or even customers. For this reason, the document should have easy-to-read content that includes an executive summary, business description, market analysis, and demand estimation, management team, description of your products or services, marketing, and sales strategy, and financial details.

Appendix A
Cover page

Company Name Business Plan

Logo

Full Company Name, LLC
Address of Company
City, State, Zip Code
Telephone Number:

Date Written:
Date of Business Plan Presentation:

Name of owner/Directors (Address, Telephone, Email)

Bankers:
Attorneys:
Auditors: